WHERE
NEVER
IS
FOREVER

WHERE
NEVER
IS
FOREVER

NEW POETRY

BY
CLAIRE BURCH

REGENT PRESS
BERKELEY. CALIFORNIA

ISBN 13: 978-1-58790-132-4
ISBN 10: 1-58790-132-3
LCCN: 2007924075

Dedicated to Mark Weiman

Manufactured in the U.S.A.
REGENT PRESS
www.regentpress.net
regentpress@mindspring.com

Part One

WHERE NEVER IS FOREVER

{ I }

So off I went
Still tilting at some windmill tilting back.
And all the windows ate the door
Or we were poor.
I don't remember much
Which keeps me on my way.

The pace I keep
Holds demon days at bay.
And hey okay
It could have been some other
Worse off way.

Last chance to catch the gold ring
Or anything.
Merry go round not found
I love you all.
Come and forget with me a little while
Like thirties songs
My mother played   my daddy sang.
The style
Was jaunty   hide all pain
Pandora's box   bagels and lox
The memories flood again.

It's not too late.
I'll meet you at the gate.
The world's our oyster still.
(We've had our fill of
The time so sad
It can't even be told.
To exit is to enter
Subway ride.)

Autumn came early.
Wan and pale
I mostly stayed indoors.
Upside down is upsy daisy
After I fell upstairs.

As soon as I knew the world was round
I wanted to flatten it.
Encourage litany
Where one and one makes three.

Under the overhang   down by the bay
Maybe I'll meet you and maybe not.
I'm just a kid with my head in the clouds.
Can't forget crowds.
All here now rise.
Friendly surprise.

Dreams and forced landings.
Mars and Venus
Point accusing finger.
Days of thirst and hunger.

Out of the frying pan   into the fire.
What is the difference between truth and error?
While lolling in some thoroughfare
I thought that I could fly.
Note my lack of logic
Hey de hey.

{ II }

The honey in the jar.
The mystery hard to say.
Where never is forever
And one and one makes three.

Not too late   not too late at all
We turned morning to night and Spring to Fall.
And that was before
Reinventing the wheel
At the time of the big bang.

Three grew over the shopping list.
What is the fate I can't request?

After the Fall we started again
Worried and wondered
And didn't know when.
These are the days of small supposes
Mine and yourses   loving phrases.

And if you climb sacred mountains
You'll know just what I mean.
Like silk road sacred mountains
Things are never what they seem.

And so and so
I thought you'd want to know
Why I didn't take that ride
Or march in that parade.

{ III }

Party of six
Riding through glaciers of ice
Seeding the sky
Pioneers of tranquility
Sleeping on layers of lace
Running in place.

Chorus of cannons
Last chance to cancel
Landed on barges
Bulging with Bibles
Seedlings and Crude Oil
Notebooks and Pencils.

Counter culture as a force of nature
Funny face fly
If you can't don't worry
Neither can I.

Not brought up on spell check I doubt my perception
My ass still stuck in my temporal lobe
Causing some havoc to hacker and dybbuk
And virus the tribe.

Lemonade smile to the end of failure.
Open the door for Helen Keller.
Cleopatra loved every long haired sailor.

We wished we were in the land of Canaan
Curse of the working class.
Lost land lives in the over under
Lucid dream of critical mass.

When first I saw that the world was broken
(Happy birthday to you)
Words floated by but never spoken
Just fade away.

Bake a cake — have a stroke — it's really all the same.
Drown or reach out for the tender rope of time.
Heaven still leaking in a covered chamber pot.
Stand up — fall down — forget your pants are wet.
Old fashioned commode on some cerebral road
I.C.U. and I love you (condition finally slowed).
Transfer to wheelchair — never really safe.
Big bang says physics. Black hole. Get a life.
Names float forgotten on a long green boat.
Who was the what? With dangerous heart rate?
What was the who? Perceived by patient's fright?
Therapy, therapy, just have hope.
Can't walk, blurred talk, honey sit and weep.
A beautiful mind poured down the kitchen drain.
What if the charge nurse can't put in a line?
I.V. — low blood pressure — dehydrated nature.
Open arterial closure with some skilled and careful suture.
Therapy, therapy, how do you do?
Learn to transfer — learn to turn — and finally tie your shoe.

{ V }

By the shores of gitchy Goomie
Dwelt a maiden Minnehaha
Looking for Hiawatha
Senseless, sad and gloomy.

Often when the sky floats by
I really think it's blue.
A hurricane in a spider web
And that was all I knew.

Jimmy stranded on Glory Street
Going to meet the Man.
Nobody Knew His Name.
Milktrain's Gone Too Long.

While in this horizontal world we stand
Small verticals still dancing to
Invisible brass band.

Well the planes went free with a memory or three
Tales of the never heard.

Save lives with passion's landing
On the helicopters grieving
Legs spread wide
Drowning in the shade.

After the Fall we started again
Worried and wondered and didn't know when.
These are the days of open and closes
New lost causes, finds and losses
Heirloom roses and eyes and noses.

And so and so
I watched the levees go.
(But I didn't take that ride
Or Mardi Gras parade.)

{ VI }

It's a long red tunnel and a thin gray line.
Skinny dipping   flood water's not fine
When we try to get
In the carpool lane.

After the Fall, what comes after?
Herd of wild elephants   tears and laughter.
These are the days of finds and losses
Abraham and Moses   long pauses.
(The Emperor of Ice Cream)

And the brief was lengthy and the trial unfair
So we lost it all but I didn't care.

It's like this old sweetie   if you want to know
Hang out somewhere where spaghetti trees grow.
The dream we live in takes its daily toll
Mosquito buzzing on a window sill.

After the Fall   we went on vacation
The apple half eaten
God mad at us still.

In spite of the flooding   we're holding the hill
But cold and hungry after the Fall.
Kissing the feet of Buffalo Bill
Red Rover go over   it's less than a mile.

{ VII }

After the Fall
Days of hugs and kisses.
Reading the mail
Eight and eight makes ten.

Scaredy cat whistle
Kissing in the dark
Ten PM at Now and Then
And Lost and Found at work.

After the Fall   hey what came after?
Chorus of chaos   tears and laughter.
These are the days   of debts and bosses
Open city and lichens and mosses.
(The Emperor of Rock and Roll)
Grass grew over Ken Kesey's vest.
Which is the one we love the most?

Payday   child's play
Pray in the yields of the soul.
Birth in the wild   cutting the cord.
(The Emperor of Burnt Toast)

Amadeus   raised in chaos
Pagan vegan   to delay us.

Clover grew over the flooded coast.
What is the fate we can't resist?

It's a long grey tunnel and a thin red line
And the dream's time coded when you pay the fine.

Don't know whether we're Slave or Boss
Land of the Found and Lost.

{ VIII }

Grief was Always   the end not near
While we tossed it all   in a gust of fear.

Ashes to Builders   future craze
Government government   lies   lies
Winter came early   mother knows best.

Go down to Heaven and count to three
This is the testing ground for Thee.
Nights of hunger and thirst.   Surprise!

Through broken city and firestorm dreams
We reach the land of Oz.

{ IX }

Three toes still lost   in an undershirt
And worried that they would unravel cloth
I lingered long in a pile of dirt
Wrote a book, had kids, you do the math.

Buried my face in my mother's skirt
And played with a duck
In a cool bird bath.

Tip top pickles and Shirley Temple
Fears and tears and a sunny dimple.

These are the things I see in court
The judge, DA and the public defender.
Hey nonny nonny, the sentence is light
Permanent press or really hard wrinkle.

Square Spare change or a rich uncle?
Hey nonny nonny   free will or fate?

Porta potty not so pretty
Used paper crumpled on the damp floor.
I'll break the law no more
Run a small convenience store.

I'd like to search and find some sweet giraffe
Still landing on the South Pole on his ass
A tipsy dipsy gypsy long ago.

But what of Adam and his partner Eve
Whose curiosity made such a mess?
Four toes now lost in a giant wave
Which of the thousands can I save?

What if the landlord of heaven
Tosses us out?
Where will we go? Is there anything I know?
Age age doesn't make us wise
Surprise those rolly bolly eyes.

{ X }

So these years later
I think of misconnected wasting days
The misbegotten and the sitcom gone.

They send our sons to Valhalla made of hate
And all those winter soldiers close the gate.
Let's go climb the cavetrees of yinyang.
Roger over and out
While government officials use their clout.

Circus tents are the only real security.
Snow stopped falling but the ocean rose
Partied our fright for six months every year.

On reflection three years later
Still chased by orange alligator
Around the BMT   (my subway station)
Dreaming in double time of a vacation.

I'm also back behind my father's store
Waiting to go to heaven
At God's mysterious whim.
Even if I don't believe in him.

Bedpan of dust.
Clean plaster cast.
Love conquers the jury.
I grow oddly weary.

Angels are whining
Seraphim complaining.
Heaven at last.
No umbrella   it's raining.

{ XI }

Dumped tomorrow   feel like shit'
Wondering who'll next be it.
Lover's animus takes over
Cover copy   scuba diver
Coloratura, soprano, tenor.

Animus possession is a
Dangerous and wanton lover.
Give time its gentle Dylan due.
See your family sitting *shiva*
(That's what happens when you're through.)

Sew buttons on your torn libido.
Careful where you plant your seedo.

See the French Lieutenant's woman.
(Fatal attraction, fatal vision.)
Carl Jung tells all
In one long session.

Age age don't make me a sage.
Rosemary, thyme, lemon and lime.
Him and me can still engage
See saw again another time.

Reupholster expectations
Purple heather unsolved crime.
If your heater is a goner
Try again another time.

If your circuit loses power
Sublimate an ounce an hour.
Think of country, God and honor.
Oink day one for wander daughters

Time heals.
Yeah yeah like birds have scales
(All those wasted orange peels).

Time sinks
While those saints are marching in.

Space smells
Take few pills
Smoke hope
Squawk, weep
Laugh   don't sniff
Smile, don't shoot
Drink bottled fruit
Juice and water
Oh my wonder wander daughters.

Stay well
See you later
Ali Allah gatorade gater
Oh my wonder wander daughter.

In the name of Zanadu
The little path is always new.
Just a moment growing out of time.

Forever some Elysian field
Way down here when the weather is mild
Bang bang the telephone is real.
No up and down is down and out
Always a performance of (or through the looking glass).
Name, alarm and eyesight, all will pass.

{ XII }

What say sweeties? Shall I try to cross
Some Donner Pass? See the wild geese? It's all the same
In fact if not in name.

Sands of Iwo Jima
Normandy sands of time
Huddled in the Ardennes
Peeing in the rain.

I've been waiting for you
In some sweet danger zone
For at the gates of trouble
Is all that's known.

What if we could ride for free? Would we?
Till birds swim   and fish fly.

I'll be with you (crunch lunch   sweet potato pie).

Packing my blue backpack
And taking off tonight
The mystery shines like Christmas.
Can't wait.

Mirror mirror in the past
To made amends I need the list.
Terror terror on the wall
Warning Columbus of the windstorn sail.
The tooth of crime is how it could have paid
But I was full of pride
And marched in my parade.

I landed on Mars with a thump
That disappearing act before and since.

I'm smiling at you
But it's still code blue   still the same.

Sliding to home   sound the alarm.
Run out of steam   looking for calm.
Heartland or east   wild west is a test.
Now there's nothing left to hide
Sweet trolley ride.
Westward the women (don't put it down).

I believe in lemonade and
Nights of heaven and parades and
Just got here (almost zonked on the road)
Felt like nothing   remembered Ma Joad.
She got through to California.

Bambi by Disney
Only when I laugh.
Keeping it together
Another kind of grief.

Home of the brave
Save and shelter me.
(I saw it in a movie once —
Coward take my coward's hand.)
Home of the brave
Save and shelter me.

In all this time it could be quite fine
Be quite fine by morning.
Take me to the mirror
Save and harbor me.
Sweet time come again
Like some confetti tree.

Out of the chaos
This whole world was formed
Fast lane transformed.
Save and harbor me.

I thought I saw you floating by
With gumdrops in your hair —
Brothers before the turn of tide
And all that sunshine near.

I thought I saw you standing there and looked again
And everything was upside down. The underside
Was so lovely like a Coney Island ride.

And then I looked again and it was there I saw
Two camels on some Adriatic shore
Around the Hebrides where ice cream grows.

Come home to heaven where the soldiers never died
And where the jazz musicians   no longer are afraid.

Take time   count to nine   getting to the river
Days of cool unreason   oh yes birds just walk
Fish fly   things change   birthday gifts to take.

Days of cool unreason
Please don't fade away.
This is the hour of the absolute
And open heart went down the street.
(There is no higher joy beyond).

We climb time and carry bags and finally we are grown.
It's a small town in the city of Heaven
To each his peach and pear is given.
In my mind you never let me down.

In the dream I have of you
The little path is always new
Just a minute rolling out of time.

Up and down is down and out
Always a performance of
Or through the looking glass.
Names alarms and crabgrass all will pass.

If smile a while to be in style
Is flying in the sun
It can't be open city if it's closed.

Honey we can wander in
The open city of the mind
At least those that are known.

If out of time to be in tune
Is flying in the sun
(At least those that are grown).

Open city take a stand
I believe in Beulah Land.
Furry feathers torn and pinioned
Still the best we've ever had.

Cold bed. Babe took off for parts unknown.
Time bursting in a spitfire green
Land sighted   come tell me when it's gone.

{ XIII }

Tall stir cry   still wooded in a pile of grass
Seeing a pool of bathers in a deer song
Lost lamb play fire on a shred of tree.

Oh salad bar wherever you are
The dust is turned to flour.
Began begat   and that is that
Is always sweet or sour.

Pause pause   oh Santa Claus
The giver and the doer.

Movers and shakers are confined
So pray for loss of power.
Throw Thy cream pies in my face
When my short time is over.

"My heaven's so high I can't get over it,
So low I can't get under it,
So wide I can't get around it,
Gotta come in by the door."

How will we know if it's heaven or hell?
Limbo or purgatory?
By the true delight and the long wait
We'll know when the spirit is here.

Yay   the amen palace   absence of malice
Walking baby home
We live in his green palace
It never will be the same.

I didn't know if the world was round
Or you were round instead.

{ XIV } A Streetcar Named Disaster

I have seen New Orleans clinging to a tower
Eighteen children on a roof.
Intelligent design? A half a million terror.
A thirsty baby's signs of ending life.
Geraldo at his network microphone
Describes the scene and cries.
Mothers and fathers in a sweaty daze —
Where were the rescuers to keep them safe?

Some trudge along in water mixed with shit.
The cisterns overflowing and not yet
Clean water, bread and milk.
Federal heart of stone
Until Geraldo fiercely shouted out
The huddled masses only stand and wait.

Thank you Geraldo. You got the President going.
Brown bodies left there still. All is not well.
What is the half mast flag exactly saying?
Body or soul.
I hear New Orleans crying
A summer's tale.

{ XV }

Two bloods converged in a wider strain
And worry I would not go insane.
I walloped my boss and whipped his ass
And poof, like a malted, he was gone.

When in cavort with Tuesdays and Chas ties
I do remember wool and snazzy tweed.
All hail Columbia. Jump the frozen hoop.
The grapes of wrath once splattered on my stoop.

When I lived in a hovel
My treble was off.
Contralto couldn't shovel.
Hard rock left me deaf.

Sit along a green fence
A locket filled with pee.
All the sky is underground
Tomorrow is today.

Nostalgia in my voice Chas
For friendship's smiling cave.
I was not a Wac or Wave
I am not now nor was ever brave.

We worried in the "good" war
Father, feather sweet good night.
That was then and now is now
Print your MacWorld cool site.

Peace is what we're fighting for
Terrorist's September date.
Upsy downsy altered state
Man's Hope is Man's Fate.
We are what we dream, Chas.

I thought of little Dee Dee twice
Pink nightie at her evening prayer.
Carpet printed with Mother Goose.
North Brother Island. Winter ice.

My brain begins to rust. Don't wait.
Catch your train or plane or boat.
We are what we weep, Chas.

The disk is in the wrong hard drive
The Internet saw the sender split
To fields below your centerfold
And dreams not ready to be told.

Spit out your watermelon seeds
And *Yahweh* we shall finally be
Caught in some Baltic old misdeeds.
I thought of little Dee Dee again
Pink nightie at her evening prayer.

Alarmed by circuses and bread
I copped the Word and hurried in
To make my tarnished spirit shine
Yahweh taking what was mine.
Pastures greener than gamblers
Thicker than thieves.
We are what we seem, Chas.

{ XVI }   MY MAIDEN NAME WAS COHEN

When in regress with visions of His ways
I all alone weep my Jewish pride.
So it might be that Heaven soon replies
Maybe our mentors and the Talmud lied?

If Heaven is now with all its small print clauses
We should not sign without a lawyer's okay.
That contract might be full of legal loopholes
That make us cry and make our hair turn gray.

What answer to breath stopping
Shrieks of despair about the baby gone
Before he could say sentences, know music.
Yahweh, if you exist, give us a sign
You had the right to take what still was mine.

Al, my father, was also ill treated by *Yahweh.*
Al's trigeminal facial neuralgia
Would start around two PM most days of his life.
"How do you feel Daddy?" I'd often say.
"Two o'clock came early today," he'd sometimes reply.

A Jewish child sits quietly in the back of the drugstore.
He'd give us milk sugar capsules to play doctor with.
"Your children are so good Doc," his customers would say.

When more is less, with fortune and fruit pies
I all alone can't sleep, remembering grief,
I pick calendulas but to my surprise
Learn only stones on Jewish graves are safe.
According to ritual. Why can't we put flowers
Like Gentiles Do? They say in Rome
Do as the Romans do.
Why *Yahweh* has these rules is beyond me.

When intersecting with remembered past
We think of seven tired angels,
Tossed to seven storms
But landing in the sun and seven Jewish babies just begun.
As open heart surgery gives us second chances
So this cloud world of arteries and veins
Severed so long ago,
Brings new defenses.
Children of children of arm branded survivors
Though safe in bed, still dream and get the shivers.

When intersecting with remembered *Yorzheits*
I use a cell phone, dial a dour deity.
So be it, be in, bee hive. Open city
Took my pale starving landsmen
And did the same to them as was done to yours, Jimmy.

"The ball I threw while playing in the park
Has not yet reached the ground."
That Fall we felt like crying in the dark
But never made a sound.

See you around, honey, see you around.

Allen Ginsberg's father Louis wrote rhymed poetry.
Allen at the end rhymed also though the content
Was always more rebel irreverent.
Oh Allen I liked your *Kaddish* better than the real one.

Well we grew up show Jews in an Italian neighborhood.
Quiet as synagogue mice my sister and I
Huddled in the back of our father's store being good.
Our father always cheerfully refunding the price of the half used
Bottle of perfume and extra strength Exedrin
To prove Jews weren't Shylocks.
While we earnestly explained to our classmates at PS 170

That borscht was made from beets
Not the blood of Christian children.

My maiden name was Cohen.
There were hundreds of us in the Brooklyn telephone directory.
My grandfather would bring his own sandwiches when he came.
We weren't kosher enough for him.

Twice a year we went down a flight of stairs
To the basement synagogue
With the sign that said PLEASE DONATE WHAT YOU CAN
TO GET US OFF THE GROUND.

My aunts all had muskrat winter coats dyed to look like mink.
V'yis ga dash v'yis ga dal
Buray puree hagorfen
Sounded like something you'd make in the blender.

Still infuriated by Kaddish I weep over episodes of ER
Like Alyosha in "The Brothers Karamazov" screaming,
"How Could He be a benevolent God who kills babies?"
If He's benevolent He's not all powerful,
If He's all powerful He's not benevolent.
Hating Him for His acts of violence. Hating the Bible.

Last Yom Kippur my mother said she had nothing to atone for.
I have hatred of God, my worst sin.
Raging, awake at three in the morning, running to the kitchen
For bread and butter my best tranquilizer.

Sleepless in Berkeley, furious at the words of Kaddish
When at the moment of loss
We're supposed to praise His name.
Only comfort in fixed form. Back to a sonnet.
Robert Lowell went bananas.
Even sonnets couldn't save him. Can they save me?

Climbing Mount Hebron
But left my boots behind.
Climbing some new Masada
Afraid of what I'll find.

Days of wrath   some primrose path
Life scribbled like a kosher grocery list
Reform pina colada
Or ortho lox twice blessed.
Yahweh You broke Your promise
Saying Father knows best.

Scaling Annapurna
My jacket torn and stained
Some memory Jerusalem of the mind.
Du wop and bo peep   sleepytime sleep.
Walk on the waters   walk on the dead sea.
Talmud and Torah
And baby makes three.

In World War Two before United Nations
We took a break and opened
Some leftover K rations.

(Please close remembered window.
Sadness too much to bear.
Skinny Jewish babies
Piled in a cattle car.)

Open hearted sorrow, swing on a broken branch.
The victims were childhood sweethearts.
He met her at a dance.
Hear the harmonic minor, may I have the honor?
(The weary ghosts of Linz.)

Light a *Yorzheit* candle at some warm family Shabbat
My maiden name was Cohen, the candle wouldn't stay lit.
Exodus seems forever, the ship arrives on time
The bus pulls into safety, we took the right plane.
The minute stays for always, as the grey times fade.
Wave to the scared survivors
On that Coney Island ride.

(It's time to live in present tense
Some disappearing act my best defense.)
Mystery unsolved. In World War Two they'd say
Bullet had your number yesterday.

What they meant was pretty clear
Father, mother, son and daughter
Sweeties I'll be there.

Mirror mirror on the past
To make amends we need the list.
Terror terror on the wall
Warning this century of the unsent mail.

The tooth of crime is how it could have been
But I didn't take that ride
Or march in that parade.

Still Waiting for Lefty
Lost in a rent strike dream.
(Things aren't ever what they seem.)
The Forties say, on a Genocide day
End of game.

I'm smiling at you but it's still Code Blue, still the same.
If the earth washes down to the flooded levee
Keep it light not heavy, forged passport, savvy?

Keep it high blood pressure and Uncle Louie.
Time is no crime. *Yahweh* knows best.
Grandma the same make me a list.

Noodle kugel and daffy down dilly
Secular, secular, holy holy.
Don't quote me   I'm saying it off the cuff.
Landmine   enough.

{ XVII }

Whose ashes are these? I think I know
A thousand Robert Frosts ago.
He wouldn't have blinked to see me here
And watch my heart fill up with snow.
These thoughts are fey and hard to keep.
You made us promises too steep
And fell from grace and cried and died.

Who turned cold eye and spoke too low
When you had nowhere else to go?
Dulled your swift smile, your heart as well.
These woods are Robert Frost's not ours.
In winter, by dim candlelight
I see your grand mal seizures still.

I'm going out to see my small wild child
Still standing by her backpack. Didn't know why.
Cruzito's Code of Honor gone to sleep.
But I have promises so deep
I could not reach them or the light that failed.

Two psyches diverged in a Robin Hood.
You could not calm them then and understand
That heroin might bring them both together.
(Too strong, too pure, the rose began to wither.)
Truths no autopsy ever said.
(In real life good is good, and blood is blood.)

Whose life is this, my broken child?
Whose China white in package sealed
Between the crosses row on row
Like Rupert Brooke three wars ago?
Thin skin, run and win
Blessings, baby smile.

Don't take the 'A' train.
Beware the white whale
It fractures with its tail.
(Icy sliver in my brain.)
And if by chance
We did our little dance.
The water sure is wide
Is what the Bible said.
The movie Code of Honor
We saw it once together.
We saw Cruzito die.

Oh heroin   oh heroin the airplane can't fly.
The worm is in the rose.
I don't knowhowor why.

Open city have pity. Water wings
Golden Gate bridge today.
Fall away sweet joy to your once cry voice
On the bus to far away.

Named now, seven faced, river beyond sea,
Ill starred, apart, signed, unblind, unmarried,
Screamed, immortal, unchanged,
Pass in grace, up some Holy Girder.
Forgiven, forgiven *buree puree almay malhuso*
(I know only three lines of *Kaddish*
But will say them for the rest of my life.)

Whose labels are these? I think I know.
My child is in Jung's river though.
In dreams I run to meet her there
Sweet end to life's last picture show.
When we saw Code of Honor
It portended
Some agony still open ended.

You were Cruzito I was Mama.
In the dark of a movie theater our fate was sealed
In this short vale of hand held docudrama.
In the movie Cruzito overdosed.
And so, as you half planned it, you did too.
Whose dead are these? I'll look and see.
You will not hear me crying though.
Like Frost my heart fills up with snow
That turns to ice as is its way.

{ XVIII }

Children on milk cartons
Missing they find
Some sand crab bitten ocean
Green ocean of the mind.

It's all a fairy story
Alarming and so gory.
(Tuesdays With Morrie
One best seller met a feller.)

Can't fast forward over the scary parts.
Roll me over in the clover —
World War Two —
After the Fall I asked you
About those Days of Wrath.
Can't even remember your answer
Some Biblical primrose path.

Listened to the heavy metal
Looking for the Emperor of no name.

Hard to find the oyster
In the after hour pearl.
In life's locked safe, in Harry Hope's saloon
No rave review by Pauline Kael.

I walked upon the water
Like I oughter while I fought her
My other self left lying in the sand.
After the Fall a dream of kindergarten
And six buns burning on a hot dog stand.

Once, insensate, I walked the ocean floor
Thinking there was a party nevermore.
As ". . . my last duchess hanging on the wall."
Begun begat begin the beguine. (God's funky free for all.)

Grandpa, my blessed daddy (Al was his name)
Sent my blessed mother birthday cards with poems
So she thought he had written Robert Browning's.
And so it goes.

Life is so dorky honey buns.   Accept it.
Run with it red rover.
Spit out the apple pit.
Prepare to smile
Before you run for cover.

{ XIX }

Into hurrah my child and yours
Are romping in some Mardi gras.
Angel and angel, wreathed in smiles
Pink processed, like in fairy tales.

I don't believe in God you know
But our dead children can't be gone.
They're laughing behind some shady gate.
It wasn't chance, it wasn't fate.

It isn't over, sweetie pie.
He who let small flowers die
Needs to be punished.
When I'm gone
Between Rupert Brooke's crosses, row on row,
I'll whip His Ass
And carry on.

Don't cry.
I never thought it through.
Some Samuel Beckett end game
And now or never
Or magic Zen
For things we can't undo
Or start again
On some star treck car wreck
Saved by Lassie and Rin tin tin.

{ XX } A BLESSING FOR THE FILMMAKER

The English Doctor
The Lady In-Patient
The Responsible Rightness of Dying
The British Banker   the English Ancient
The Comparable Sightness of Seeing

The American Producer
The Budget   the Budget
The Responsible Parties are Fleeing

The London Contingent
They is or they isn't?
The Haphazard Silence of Needing

Remember Suspense?
It worked for Saul Zaentz
The Inoperable Myth of Agreeing

The English Doctor
The Despairing Patient
The Details involved in the Screening
The American Producer
The Hurry   the Worry
The Passion   the Vision   the Bearable Darkness of Sighing

The English Paramedic
The Latest Sensation
The Funding   the Dollars and Cents
The Hurried and Worried Saul Zaentz
The Writer's Defense

The Unflappable Funders
The Actors   the Extras   the Boy Wonders
The Sundance, and Cannes, the next Screening

The Pissing and Moaning
The Work never Ends

The British Mailman
The English Accent
The Impossible Goal of just Resting

The Busy Producer
The Mind on the Run
The Movie the Movie   the Contracts
The Concept   the Shoot just Begun
Director   Director   Work Faster
Work Faster to Win

The English Nurse
The Backers Impatient
The Comparable Whiteness of Bleaching
For Better or for Worse

Saul Zaentz is reaching
The Bankable Stars still Beseeching
(The Molecular Content of Screeching)
The Disreputable Aspect of Praying
The Retirement Income
The Hilarious of Highness

And over the Cast hovers Cloud Number Nine or Disaster
The English Backer
The American Producer

So now in present tense
Que pasa Saul Zaentz?
It makes so little sense
To still be going faster.

{ XXI }

Payday   Child's play
Will the passion go away?

Two blew over Ken Kesey's List
Which was the One he Loved the Best?
Birth of Three Warriors   Cut the Cord
Live by the Lost and Found   Die by the Sword.
At Work   Hard Work   in the Yields of the Horde

Shoo fly or Mosquito   the Wafer the Host
Fly south Mosquito! Gold Coast, Burnt Toast!
Sorrow or Fun   Amadeus or Chaos
Last of the Just   Heretic or Pious
Rust into Passed   Predict into Guessed
Producer   Director   the Cream of the Cast
The Unstoppable Long Stream of Peeing.

If the Funding flies South
Remember back East it is Raining
While Saul Zaentz   in Present Tense
Prepares for Another Screening.

{ XXII }

When hate crime last in a bombscare loomed
Then and only, a skinny boy
Slipped on fresh graves for the newly doomed.
Speechless in shock, we didn't know why.

Where were the gone when the World Trade fell?
Down went black in a slam of smoke.
Heart broke twice when a single arm
Lay in the rubble, swollen and still.

I'm staying in. I saw the darkened sky
Through memory's wind crushed window. It's so hot
It burns you when you think of it and cry.

Everyone's son and wife and husband and daughter
Still missing. Let's rush down to check the list.
We have a flyer with the tear stained photo.
Please call if you should see them. We have hope.

I just gave birth to triplets. I must cope
With being alone to raise them. Rest in peace.
The body parts are smoldering in a heap
And love lies burning through the fire truck mist.

When if ever the firemen died
Brave as babies who touch the stove
Innocent still but now afraid
They learn at the end about true love.
Hijackers gone we are one nation.
What was the cause they died to save?
The building gone, we are still alive.
Feels like an Arctic space station.

When terrorists took the World Trade
Three thousand gone in a jump cut fade.

Part Two

NOW I AM BLIND

{ XXIII }

Now I am blind I see the sky open
Like curtains in a room.
And stars like candies with their wrapper gone
And moons and suns on every glimmer corner.
I rarely saw such beauty in the days
When I still had my eyes.
To be blind is to be at an art opening
(Matisse Matisse Van Gogh Van Gogh)
Surprise surprise.

And some disconnect ·
Can make us cry or laugh in awe
That eyes that cannot see reality
Now often see something better.

In the beginning was the land and sky.
Then funny animals and millions of years later
People, and after people, libraries
To save their stuff.
The Bancroft Library
Has gobs of stuff that people want to save.
I want to save my stuff too.
The data reproduces by itself.
A book makes books, manuscripts the same.
Tapes give birth to tapes and the library overflows
Until the tsunami rolls in one sunny day
And washes it away.

Roll out the sheets of eyes.
Wind them up to read the data base.
Ain't this world a strange and funny place?

Now I am blind I see great foaming oceans
In every glass of water.
High mountains whiter than cream
Lost cities in every puddle
Jeweled buildings on every street
Ebbing fires in the middle
Rise up before me at the touch of morning.
Baskets of flowers hang from every window
And all the world is silver lined, and dreams
Turn real and shimmer and shake now I am blind.

{ XXIV }

My flowers die I know not how and why.
I always water them.
The tooth fairy came
Let them spare change but did not water them.
And so they fade.
Everything fades.
Our cheekbones turn to powder.
We put our quarter in life's parking meter.
Oh Bancroft Library and other symbols
Of keeping the data where anyone can see it.

My muscles ache with laughing at God's jokes.
Who are we?
How shall we wander home?
Summer gone.
No humming bird tonight
Or corn remembering its stalk
And lazy days and summer talk.
One Labor Day when working at my task
I turned and in a vision saw
Robert Frost's calf.
It was standing by the author and so young
It tottered when Frost's cow licked it with her tongue.
Well I forget the rest.

Three camels that I never met before
Watch the parade.
A thousand children march
And wave their letter banners in the rain.

{ XXV }

I'm going in to catch a falling star
That wandered on my pillow.
It will squeak and tickle.
Its sharp edges make me laugh.
A little fun goes far.

I'm going in to find a baby shoe
Remembering my little son and how it was
For that grand fourteen months he was on earth.

I hate you God or fate.
That baby never hurt a fly.
He had blonde ringlets and a shining smile and often
We played hide the matzoh and it wasn't even pass over.

Quack like a duck in pink champagne —
Now I am blind I see new sights.
I see great cities in their sleep
When lilacs last on Walt Whitman grew.

When if ever my mind cleared
Bury my knee in the stratosphere.
Rope of tomorrow tied in a knot
Oh see pink worlds gone gray in the light.

{ XXVI }

Now I am blind I see a soldier smile
At being given Christmas fucking dinner in his trench.
The time is tangled like spaghetti now
That I am blind.
A fire island of the fate   unkind
Is sort of how the dead sea rose.
Hey join the flashlight of the free
The lantern of the brave.

What is the cross too large to bear?
He would not see me standing there
To watch the world fill up with snow
When honey, we've no place to go.

Here's what I see now I am blind —
London when Mary Queen of Scots reigned —
An afternoon with Einstein, pickled lace —
I do not think that I shall go there twice.

Blindness is kind to me. (Those daily papers
I'll never read again, the advertisements
For things we'll never want, the distractions
I'll never have again.)
I tamper with eternity, and think
I can persuade it to bother us no more
Than a hundred years from now and then just end.

I see six seasons now that I am blind.
The Bancroft Library wants my correspondence.
I wonder why I am not famous or rich?
I'll sail away. I'll smile. I'll light a match.

Though blind I am still driven.
When I die will I go to heaven?

Lost lantern on a scarlet fireside
When lilacs last in Walt Whitman died.

A sound of weeping at the Donner Pass —
Flames and swift running (one can only guess).

I'm going in to find a feathered fern
With leaves so dry they make a sailor cry,
Where late is always soon and angels fly
Like swarms of bees that make my blind eyes widen
In wonder at the view.

It's morning now. I am a stone's throw
From Helen Keller insights.
Sight is so strange when wonderland breaks through.

{ XXVII }

Now I am blind I see a rolling sea
A single day away.
When Bing Crosby crooned
In the movies, then if ever
Good deeds rang up on the register like sales
While we just ran for cover.

A quarter pound of old time religion and top forty.
My head's on backwards splash it with yon hose.
And while you're up, get me a cherries jubilee.
I always coveted flaming food and funding
But also served who only stand and wait.

Just before my first date
My mother looked at me and said,
"We should have got the other dress."
And so it goes.
Who know why or when?
My mind can focus on some universe.
I'm going in to phone my children there.
My best success, they are my heart of lightness.
They have their children now and time runs fast.

Down at the dinghy Salinger cried
When if ever grow perfect skies?
Mother went out to the green world
Found me a baby, surprise surprise.
These are the dreams of lemon cake
Love on a raft and set in our ways.
We broke all records for hundred yard sprint
Fell on our face and became a saint.

These are the nights of verbs and clauses
Lilies in the valleys and smiling faces.
Once while sleepwalking I ate an onion,
Became the tenth in a Yiddish *minyan*.

I never saw a silent sound
Or heard a grocery snore,
But know that if a ghost's around
It's one I knew before.

{ XXVIII }

And all I am is a woman
Mooning about what's for dinner.
Winter is a coming in.
Count your blessing don't cry.
Hyperventilate with joy.

Calibrate some Appian Way.
Eat a bagel every day.
Line each alphabet with hay.

Enter a Bancroft Library curator looking pale.
"The library has been moved," one curator says.

"We relocated in a brothel
Containing Billie Holliday's mother
That splendid singer saved."
"Wait," said another curator.
"We would have to evict the poor woman
To house our splendid artifacts."
"What a conflict," Jack London replies
From one of the books that came tumbling down
When they moved.
The other curator had another suggestion
For where they could put their books
And a happy ending was achieved.

Books on my mind —
Unless the letters are so big
The page is read in teeny bits.
But still the mountains that I see
In dishes filled with spinach pie
And all the gold that runs down bread
And butter turned to armies of peace
Now turns me on.

I see huge cornucopias of fruit
Seven feet high in every cup.
And kiddo, see the ocean there
In half a dozen cookie crumbs.
Well curators, your retrofit
Will house with honor a glimpse of then
And now beyond a farmers doubt
That spring will come when winters past.

I have a mind now I am blind
To sit and watch a faucet drip.
The audio tells me what to think
When in line at some old bank.

What I see no one can see
The privilege is mine I find.

{ XXIX }

The Bancroft Library had an exhibit
At the University Art Museum.
History where there is never snow
And one and one makes seven.

I'm going up to see the tidal wave
That floods the beach and makes us all afraid.
That ocean is so dangerous we run
Back on the whitened sand and find a friend.
Good morning Sunshine honey, you bring your lunch.
We eat an Eskimo pie we sit upon a bench.
A laser caught your eye.

What next dear heart, I don't know what to say.
And so it ends. Let's be friends.

One day I caught a baby in a net
And raised it to a doctor. I was proud.
My orange heart still bleeds for those long gone.
Open the angel wings and carry on.

There was no telling and there is no way.
Those broken hearts that shake at old losses
Can never heal but keep the demons at bay.
Horizon lines are blurred now I am blind.

Not enough ritual.
Maybe I should hotfoot it to a *mikvah?*
No. I'll go to the
Bancroft Library instead.
I'll fall asleep in a book and become
A character.
The sun sets regularly at Rago's house.
Should I stir fry, live or die, bake a shoo fly pie?

Mommy what's a pie?
A pie is a poem child.
It contains flour and water, berries and sugar,
Sometimes molasses,
Profits and losses.

When lilacs last in Walt Whitman bloomed
Then as always my heart stopped.
(Fibrillation is no joke.)

Down by the dinghy hide and seek
Follow the trip at fractured hip.
This is the gift I give to thee.

UPS or Fed Ex and more
Lilacs tall by the back door.
Where is the land of Lassie and Oz?
Never is now (probably was).
I'm going back to find my memory bag.
(Drive to forever in a heavy fog.)

Old friends all gone I light a *yorzheit* candle
And evening rides to visions of jolly heaven.
I'm coming in to meet the quick brown fox
That jumped over
The first black hole
When one and one made seven.

A pup tent of World War Two fades from my view.
The world is too much with us late and soon.
We walk around the flowers at high noon.
Be civil civilization, remember the Alamo.

{ XXX }

I'm going in to find
Small pancakes. Where's the syrup?
Watt Whitman arrives and eats seven.
Hey hey, to each a gift is given.
Mine was the whitened ash of yesterday.
I know not how or why.

Good morning Sunrise, the sky is falling.
Peel the orange, God willing.
The Bancroft Library is sad
To see its shiny trophies fade.
This is the truth so help me Mom
Baby needs a new pair of governments.

Helen Keller went to heaven.
There she finally learned to *daven*.
Yahweh came by and wished her well.
Bessie Smith sang "My Bill"
And Life was swell.
Get thee to a nunnery honey.
It calibrates the mind.
I'm seeing things I never saw before.
Makes it OK or half okay.
Would I have had it another way?
You bet. To have my old eyes back
Would make me quack like some nocturnal duck.

I judge the heroine's Festivals of Heaven.
Helen Keller won.
Her trophy is covered with eyes.
She smokes pot in eternity.
It helps her relax she says.

Who knows where the 60s went?
Break out the champagne. No, not in plastic glasses.
What's the world coming to?
I'm coming in to fix the fire wire
That ties camera to computer (it often doesn't do it).
It's my swan song.
My life's work
Stretches before me and around my neck.

See those captured fragments of the street
Where throwaway people walk, beg, spare change,
Light cigarettes, drink beer, smoke purple haze.
Will the filmed records of their lives
Turn to powdery mildew? What gives?
Ashes to ashes, mother know best
What is the thing we fear the most?

The Bancroft Library   save it from fire.
I'd hide it all but I don't know where.

I see great cities in the dirt.
A thousand towers and open spaces
Mango eyes in a thousand faces.

{ XXXI }

What I wrote last just got erased.
I guess I hit the wrong thing twice.
This modern world is mine to touch.
I do not like it very much.

Oh by the way the Bancroft Library
Just kind of came to me and gee
They sure were nice.
Nothing much happened.
There was talk
Of preservation of the Archive.
But they've got all this other stuff to save.

Okay the ambulances were real.
Death visited every day.
My head's on backwards.
Let it spin for a while.

Yay the bullet didn't have my number.
Given more time I seethe and simmer,
Try to last till the next Mardi Gras.
These are the days of hybrid seeds
Peaceful peaceniks and brass band parades.

Oh by the way
My sour etcetera uncle Bernie
Could and what is more
Didn't know what we were waiting for.
(Tip of the hat to ee cummings.)

Now I am blind I joke a lot
And as for shit am full of it.
You will not see me weeping here
Or watch my eyes fill up with snow.

I have a tendency now I am blind
To ride some long lost loop de loop
And that way find
A Ferlinghetti of the mind.

Oh boy here I am back online
But everything's not fine.

Hide the cold fact
That all is not well on my street.
Telegraph Avenue and Peoples Park
Baby still needs a new pair of governments.

Now I am blind I hear a roaring sea
And amethysts float over me and splash.
My eyes burn with amethyst dust.
It's oddly pleasant and tickles while I rest.
Meantime the Bancroft Library faces another crisis.
Unable for reasons of conscience to evict Billie Holliday's
Mother from the brothel and take over the space, the
Library has to trim its collection so it will fit into the
Smaller space found. It decides to divest itself of the
Correspondence of Claire Burch and donates the collection
To the neighborhood Goodwill.

A passing artist named Jeff Koons sees it, takes it home,
Sprays it white and uses it as the teeth in a twelve foot
Puppy dog which is installed at Lincoln Center opposite
Another Jeff Koons sculpture.

It was not the Library's fault.
It was caught in a dilemma.
Evict Billie Holliday's mother or divest.

This indeed is the dilemma faced by modern man.
Well, go and catch a mandrake root.

Gild with gold a bumblebee.
(I cannot read I cannot see.
Try me again some other day.)
A fire island of the blind
A sound of weeping at the Donner Pass.
(History is such a mess.)

{ XXXII }

If I am born will the world die
And dinosaurs all go away?
I am not now and never was pumpkin pie.
Now I am blind hey hey!

The Chicago Manual of Style
Has little to offer me nowadays.
(Not that I sell pencils on the subway.)

Haunted by dreams of the Bancroft Library
I fall asleep counting ephemera.
I'm flying up to count the bob tailed squirrels
That gather on my frontal lobe these days.
(They are immune to guilt and are heartfelt.)

Seeking to snooze at the library
I crawl into a display case,
Sleep in literary peace,
Turn into acid free paper
With one small coffee stain.
Well that was then and orange now is now.

If I get sick will the Bay Bridge explode?

{ XXXIII }

God of the science hot or cold
God of the mass of conscious fire
Broken unbroken, ancient and young
Never to know right from wrong.
Culture clashes and so and so.

God of the science when it failed
Science religion, coin or token?
Science mistaken, train derailed
Fourth dimension, space and time.
Charles Townes laser what does it prove?
God of Physics the pain still mild
Iron lung breathing where real lung failed.

Bertrand Russell said all is accident.
God of the fire "The Iceman Cameth"
Stand at the gate, the global threat
Patience patience, not yet not yet.

Tomorrow is yesterday only twice.
God and religion Olympic race.
Science religion six and seven.
Justice, injustice, limbo, heaven.

Here in the world of peaceable kingdom
Sand of forever, fire and ice
Nobel Prize, first laser, religion for peace
Rational rational, winning the race.
Santayana knew it centuries ago
Science, religion, the how and why.
Reconcile, reconcile, all children's play.

John Lilly floats in a lonely tank.
God or Epson salts didn't let him sink.

{ XXXIV }

I'm going up to find a small giraffe
That's sitting by its father.   It's so cold
It quivers when this little song is sung.
I shan't be Robert Frost, you shan't too.
Blind now I see some Bancroft Library of the mind
Along a pathway I can find.
The books and memorabilia swim before me
Like channels on our turned off Comcast cable.

You will not find me crying though
I've miles to go before I slow.
These woods are Frostwrite dark and dank
I've miles to go before I zonk.

{ XXXV }

I am falling in to rent a diamond ring
And put it on a statue.
Its so wide I view it with much pride
And rent a TV just to see it.
Honey, look out, the world is falling down
Like in Our Town.
I dreamed I was dancing with Astaire or was it Gene Kelly?
Ain't life both goofy hour and holy?

{ XXXVI }

Dear Mark who monitors my pills
And reads to me my credit card bills.
Once long ago I looked and found
A sentence in a paragraph
That said that love is like a laugh.
We've had a good run.
The tide is coming in.
Who needs sand castles? Let's go wading.

"Ms. Burch is a wonderful "Berkeley Institution." For over 20 years, she has used her camera and her pen to document the plight of homeless people in our community. She is respected for her skills as a filmmaker and for her deep commitment to improving our society."

— TOM BATES, *Mayor of Berkeley, CA*

"I am aware that these awards (from California Arts Council) are granted only to those fine artists who have made outstanding artistic contributions to their communities. On behalf of Senate District Nine, I would like to commend you for your commitment to excellence and thank you for sharing your work with others."

— NICHOLAS C. PETRIS, *CA State Senate*

"Over the last several decades Claire Burch, perhaps unique among social documentarians, has given voice to the hidden cries, human struggles and often hard won wisdom that emanates from the streets of all our cities. She's offered understanding to those that we avert our eyes from and she's humanized the misunderstood. Documenting the hard, mercenary and uncaring social realities at the end of the twentieth century, Claire Burch fearlessly offers us a view into a cracked mirror of the American dream. Issues far too important to ignore come to vivid and insistent life in Claire's incisive and empathetic investigations. Her work needs to be seen by the many, not the few."

— STEVEN STARR, *Filmmaker, New York, NY*